Robert the Bruce

History Nerds

Published by History Nerds, 2022.

While every precaution has been taken in the preparation of this book, the publisher assumes no responsibility for errors or omissions, or for damages resulting from the use of the information contained herein.

ROBERT THE BRUCE

First edition. June 8, 2022.

Copyright © 2022 History Nerds.

ISBN: 979-8215222157

Written by History Nerds.

Also by History Nerds

Celtic History
Ireland

Great Wars of the World
World War 1
World War 2
The Napoleonic Wars: One Shot at Glory
The Serbian Revolution: 1804-1835
Peace Won by the Saber: The Crimean War, 1853-1856
The Fiery Maelstrom of Freedom
The Wars of the Roses

Irish Heroes
Grace O'Malley: The Pirate Queen of Ireland
William Butler Yeats: Nobel Prize Winning Poet
Scáthach
Finn McCool

The History of the Vikings
Vikings
Longships on Restless Seas

The Rise and Fall of Empires
Rome: The Rise and Fall

World History
The History of the United Kingdom
The History of Ireland
The History of America
The History of Scotland
The History of Wales

Standalone
Robert the Bruce
William Wallace: Scotland's Great Freedom Fighter

Robert the Bruce: Hero of Scotland

A great nation *needs* a great leader. Just like a ship needs a capable captain, so does a proud and sovereign nation need a competent king to lead it through the tumultuous waves of history. Alas, history taught us that capable leaders are not always readily available. Scotland's history led its people through many a dark passage: even from its earliest prehistory, this proud nation suffered at the hands of conquerors and invaders. From the Vikings to the Normans, and the English - everyone wanted to reign over proud and wild *Alba*. In the late 1200s and early 1300s, however, the people of Scotland finally stood up and sought the light of freedom: they led a series of wars that would gain them their independence. Many leaders and commanders appeared during this time, all of them leaving their trace on history. However, only one emerged as *"King of the Scots"* and led the nation to its coveted independence. That man is the famed Robert the Bruce, a national hero of Scotland and one of its most renowned warriors.

Hailing from a noble Scottish family, Robert the Bruce was hailed as one of the best warriors and knights in the whole of Europe. A King's grandson, he laid his claim to the throne of Scotland and stood firmly by it. And throughout Scotland's struggle, he was involved in the key events of the era. His life was full of ups and downs, events and intrigues - and many glorious battles. In this book we will take a detailed look into the life and times of Robert the

Bruce and will explore the impact of his achievements on the broader history of Scotland. Here is a tale of true kingship!

Chapter I

Before we delve deep into the life history of Robert the Bruce, a special word of note is needed. The names of the Bruce family can be rather confusing for every reader, so take special care. The confusion arises because of the family names of the Bruces: they are all names Robert! Fathers, sons, grandson: all are named Robert the Bruce, and are only distinguished by their "regnal" numbers. In this case, Robert the Bruce can be seen as the 7th in his line and is also distinguished by a different spelling of the surname: where he is cited as "the Bruce," his predecessors are usually cited as "de Brus," their original ancestral surname. And now, with that out of the way, we can start from the very roots!

What are the origins of the "Bruce" family? It is a wonderful way to start the story of Robert the Bruce by exploring the origins and the roots of his noble family. After all, by the time of Robert the Bruce's adolescence, this family was one of the most prominent in Scotland and had a key role to play in its politics. So how did it become so influential after all? Clan Bruce, known in Scottish Gaelic as "Brùs," is a Lowlands Scottish Clan. The official records state that this clan originates from the Flemish surname, "de Bruce," likely derived from the lands of Bruges that are today in Belgium. Another theory states that this surname is in fact of French (Norman), origin, and was originally "de Brus" or "de Bruis" and originated from the eponymous town of Brix in Normandy. This would certainly indicate that the clan has origins with Norman feudal lords that were allowed to hold lands and titles in Medieval Scotland. A disputed claim states that one of the nobles that served under the Norman leader, William the Conqueror, was in fact a man named "Robert de Brix," and that he was the clan's early progenitor. Some indications might exist that such a man fought on the Norman side at the famed Battle of Hastings, but no confirmation of the fact exists. Nevertheless, the line of descent that can be traced with certainty is one that originates with Robert I de Brus, 1st Lord of Annandale. This Anglo-Norman Lord came to England in 1106 and has been noted as a companion of King David I of Scotland. Although originally based in England, de Brus accompanied Prince David northwards into Scotland, where the latter sought to reclaim his kingdom. From this man onwards, the Bruces were known as Lords of Annandale and a powerful noble family that was continually on the rise to prominence. All this paved the way towards the rise of the future King of Scots, or Robert the Bruce that interests us.

Chapter II

Not much is known with certainty about the birth date and birthplace of Robert the Bruce. Tradition states - and it is most likely the truth - that he was born at Turnberry Castle, a sea-fort situated in Southern Ayrshire. This was for long the seat of the ancient Earldom of Carrick, which then belonged to his mother. The date of his birth is largely agreed to have been July 11th, 1274, AD. However, some later sources, notably a late 14th century English chronicler, Geoffrey of Swinbroke, stated that Robert was in fact born in a former English royal manor of Writtle in Essex. Still, it should be noted that an error likely surrounds this matter, as Robert's father, Robert VI, was in fact the one born in Writtle estates in Essex. As we mentioned earlier, Robert's father was also a Robert, styled as de Brus, 6th Lord of Annandale, while his mother was Marjorie, the Countess of Carrick. One of ten children from that union, Robert the Bruce inherited by birth some truly lofty titles and estates that the Bruces had acquired across generations. Not only would he inherit the Lordship of Annandale that belonged to the family, but also the Earldom of Carrick from his mother's side. Furthermore, he inherited a royal lineage, as he was a fourth great-grandson of the famed and successful Scottish King, David I. It was this lineage that would later give him a great upper hand in the struggle for the vacant Scottish throne. And so it was that, merely through the benefits of his noble birth, Robert the Bruce would come to hold the lands across Scotland and England: in the former he held lands in Aberdeenshire and Dundee, besides his ancestral Annandale lordship, while in the latter he had significant estates in Durham,

Essex, Cumberland, Middlesex, Northumberland, and Yorkshire. County Antrim in Ireland was also a part of his familial estates.

It should not, of course, come as a surprise to find out that history does not remember a lot about the childhood years of Robert the Bruce. As a child of significantly wealthy nobles, he would have undoubtedly had a quality upbringing, and would have spent his youth in the family's estates both in Scotland and England. As was the practice at the time, the noble education was likely oriented towards useful practices: masters would have been gathered from across the realm to tutor Robert and his brothers in the arts of swordsmanship, jousting, horse riding, hunting, and the courtly behavior that befits nobles. Furthermore, they would have acted as pages in their father's household. This was an important period where young nobles would learn all that there is to be learned about the practices at the court. Today we know Robert the Bruce as an exceptional warrior - one of the best of his time. This fact could tell us that in his youth, a skilled teacher was employed to instruct the boy in the matters of war and associated skills. Some sources state that this could have been a seasoned veteran knight and commander that belonged to the retinues of Robert's grandfather who went on the Crusades. Either way, it was clear that Robert the Bruce received fantastic military tutoring in his childhood, which would be clearly seen in his adulthood and his many military achievements. All in all, Robert was groomed from an early age to be an adequate heir to his father's estates, and a worthy new Lord of Annandale - which he certainly was, and more.

Another part of Robert's growing up was most likely the practice of fosterage. This ancient custom has been present in Gaelic lands - chiefly Ireland and Scotland - for many centuries before that. It was an important part of growing up and served to teach young boys and girls some very valuable lessons in life. Robert and his brothers had been likely fostered to their kindred families, allied clans, or septs. These could have been families such as Carruthers, Boyd, Torthorwald, Corrys, Fleming, Bosco, and others. The custom of fosterage goes back a long, long time, and it was usually reserved for the poorer families with a lot of children. If we consider the fact that Robert was just one of ten children, it should not be surprising that even the powerful Lords of Annandale relied on their lesser kinsmen to foster their numerous children. It served not only to teach children common skills of a household, but to strengthen the bond between two allied kins and families. Interestingly, the custom survived in the Hebrides of Scotland for quite a long time, up until the late 1700's. One account from that period perfectly describes it and shows us that the Lord of Annandale could have certainly benefited from sending his children - Robert especially - to his lesser kinsmen.

"There still remains in the Islands, though it is passing fast away, the custom of fosterage. A Laird, a man of wealth and eminence, sends his child, either male or female, to a tacksman, or tenant, to be fostered. It is not always his own tenant, but some distant friend that obtains this honour; for an honour such a trust is very reasonably thought. The terms of fosterage seem to vary in different islands. In Mull, the father sends with his child a certain number of cows, to which the same number is added by the fosterer. The father appropriates a proportionable extent of ground, without rent, for their pasturage. If every cow brings a calf, half belongs to the fosterer, and half to the child; but if there be only one calf between two cows, it is the child's, and when the child returns to the parent, it is accompanied by all the cows given, both by the father and by the fosterer, with half of the increase of the stock by propagation. These beasts are considered as a

portion, and called Macalive cattle, of which the father has the produce, but is supposed not to have the full property, but to owe the same number to the child, as a portion to the daughter, or a stock for the son. Children continue with the fosterer perhaps six years, and cannot, where this is the practice, be considered as burdensome. The fosterer, if he gives four cows, receives likewise four, and has, while the child continues with him, grass for eight without rent, with half the calves, and all the milk, for which he pays only four cows when he dismisses his Dalt, for that is the name for a foster child."

All of this tells us that the upbringing of Robert the Bruce was not strictly Anglo-Norman, as was often supposed. It was - most simply put - varied and included great influences from the Scottish Gaelic cultures. Because of this "multicultural" upbringing, it is reasonable to say that Robert the Bruce likely spoke three languages very early on in his life. The first would have been Scottish Gaelic, the second was the aristocratic Anglo-Norman language, and the third was the early form of the widely spoken Scots language. And of course, because of his noble birth, Robert would have likely possessed a certain amount of knowledge of Latin, which was mostly related to church matters and charter lordship. Of course, through Latin, Robert would have had access to further studies and deeper knowledge, this time related to law, politics, philosophy, and history. Without a doubt, all of these aspects worked greatly to enhance Robert's abilities as a young noble and a future leader of men. Several medieval sources that write of him tell us that he was well versed in many things, and a very educated man. It is said that in 1306, Robert the Bruce "read aloud" to his supporters and recited from memory the chivalric tales of Charlemagne and Fierabras. He would also speak of historic subjects, such as the conflict of Hannibal and Rome. It is also said that Robert *"used continually to read, or have read in his presence, the histories of ancient kings and princes, and how they conducted themselves in their times, both in wartime and in peacetime; from these he derived information about aspects of his own rule."*

Furthermore, there are contemporary documents that point to Robert's early literacy. One briefing from roughly 1364 indicates that Robert the Bruce and his siblings enjoyed substantial education and tutoring in several key spheres of medieval upbringing. Of course, much of Robert's early multi-layered education and varied upbringing (and his speaking of at least three languages), was owed to the different estates that the Bruce family owned, and the family's traveling between them. One was Turnberry Castle in Ayrshire, the likely birthplace of Robert, and the household nearest to the Gaelic-speaking Scottish isles. There was then the Lochmaben Castle, today in Dumfries and Galloway, as well as Loch Doon Castle within Carrick. Of course, there were also the estates in England, where Robert undoubtedly spent time in childhood also. All of this helped establish young Robert as a multi-faceted and able young aristocrat. Interestingly some leading historians that dealt with the life of Robert the Bruce, chiefly Penman and Barrow, propose a theory that young Robert also spent some time at the court of the English King Edward. By age 12, Robert was eligible to begin training for full knighthood, and possibly spent time with some English noble families, such as the de Clares of Gloucester. However, the medieval author, Sir Thomas Grey, in his influential chronicle Scalacronica, writes that Robert the Bruce, at age 18 (in 1292) was a *"young bachelor of King Edward's Chamber"*. There is, however, no significant evidence of Robert ever being present at the English Royal court.

One of the earliest documented appearances of Robert the Bruce in public events was the solemn gathering at Dunfermline Abbey in Fife, alongside his grandfather and father, and many other peers of the realm. The occasion was, alas, rather solemn: it was the funeral of King Alexander III, who died on March 19th, 1286, after an unfortunate fall from a horse. He was 12 at the time, and it is likely that the solemn and noble event left a profound impression on the youth. Whether or not he was aware of the growing tensions amongst the present nobles, is not known. But the tensions were certainly there: between the Bruce Lords of Annandale on one hand, and John Balliol and his Comyn family allies on the other. With the death of Alexander III, it is possible that Robert's grandfather - Robert V (known also as "Robert the Competitor") - considered the growing possibility of the Bruce family claim to the Scottish throne. This was due to the fact that the late Alexander's children predeceased their father: young Prince David died around 1281 at age 8, Princess Margaret died in 1283 aged 22, and Prince Alexander died in 1284 at age 19. And now with the death of the King in 1286, the future of the realm was on a slippery precipice.

However, the first documented mention of young Robert the Bruce (Robert VII), can be traced to a list of witnesses to a signing of a charter. This charter was issued by Alexander Og MacDonald, Lord of Islay, (Alasdair Óg Mac Domhnaill), sometime around 1284 or 1285. Also on this list was Robert's father, many lesser Gaelic notaries from Carrick, the Bishop of Argyll, a Kintyre clerk, and the Vicar of Arran.

Chapter III

By the time he was sixteen years of age, young Robert the Bruce could have already been seen as an adult and an able heir to his noble house. Either way, it was around this time that new political events broke out in Scotland, most notably the death of young Margaret, the Maid of Norway, in 1290. She was to inherit the kingdom's throne, and her death left it vacant. What ensued was the Great Cause, and the sixteen-year-old Robert the Bruce was competent enough to enter the political stage boldly, representing his familial interests. Just two years later, in 1292, Robert's mother, Marjorie the Countess of Carrick, died. Upon her death, her husband transferred Carrick to his eldest son, Robert. In that same year, the English King Edward I awarded the vacant Scottish Crown to John Balliol, the chief of the rivals of the Bruce family. A relatively obscure figure in Scotland's politics up to that point, John Balliol had a valid claim to the throne as he was the great-great-great-grandson of Scottish King David I. As soon as Balliol became King, the grandfather of Robert the Bruce - Robert V - stepped down from his position as Lord of Annandale, in favor of his son, Robert VI. In turn, Robert VII (Robert the Bruce), becomes the Earl of Carrick. This was done as to protect the Bruce family claim to the throne, and soon after, young Robert the Bruce was becoming a strong player in Scotland's fragile political scene. However, even after Balliol became King, the English monarch Edward I continued to exert his authority over Scotland, as was his plan from the get-go. This caused very strained relations between the two kingdoms, as England had for centuries pretensions over its northern neighbor.

The overall situation between the two kingdoms began to deteriorate rapidly, and the Bruce family - Robert with them - had to choose which side to support, and to look after their own interest first and foremost. Because of this, the Bruces supported the English King Edward against their rival, the new Scottish King John Balliol and his chief allies - the Comyn family, which was also the chief rival of the Bruces. Most importantly, the Bruces chose this side for two reasons: first, they saw Balliol as a usurper to the throne, as they considered their claim more legitimate. Secondly, they owned a lot of estates in England, which they would undoubtedly lose if they were to support the wrong side. The English King Edward continued his series of serious provocations against the Scottish crown and the King *he* placed on the throne. One of the first such incidents was a demand by Edward that King John Balliol was to appear personally before the English Parliament and answer for the charges brought against him by the Earl of Fife, MacDuff. Furthermore, he demanded that the nobles of Scotland all provide military service for England's war against France. Refusing this, the Scots formed an alliance with France, which would last for centuries and become known later on as the "Auld Alliance".

Robert the Bruce and his family continued their struggle for a claim they considered just. Their political rivals, the Comyn family, dominated the Scottish council, and acted in the name of King John Balliol. To that end, they summoned the Scottish nobles to a meeting that was to be held at a place called Caddonlee. The Bruces straight out refused this and had to temporarily withdraw from Scotland. The Comyns promptly seized their ancestral familial estates in Annandale and Carrick, instead granting them to John Comyn, the 3rd Earl of Buchan. The Bruces, exiled, had to seek refuge with the

English King, who greeted them and appointed Robert Bruce as the commander of Carlisle Castle, sometime in late 1295.

It was around this time that we first hear about Robert the Bruce's first marriage. This occurred in 1296, when he was roughly 22 years old. His bride was one Isabella of Mar, a daughter of the Earl of Mar, Domhnall I. The girl was, judging by historic accounts, around 18 years old at the time. This union, sadly, did not last. Young Isabella died soon after, roughly 19 years old, most likely during or after childbirth. She did, however, deliver Robert the Bruce's first child, a daughter - Marjorie Bruce. Marjorie Bruce would go on to marry the influential Walter Stewart, the Steward of Scotland, and their son would eventually come to rule as King Robert II of Scotland. Robert remarried just a few years later, this time to a girl 10 years younger than him, one Elizabeth de Burgh. She was the daughter of one of the most powerful Norman nobles in Ireland at the time, the famed "Red Earl" - Richard Óg de Burgh, 2nd Earl of Ulster and 3rd Baron of Connaught. This indicates that Robert the Bruce was seen as a very fine and suitable match for this Earl's daughter, and that with this marriage his influence and power only increased.

The conflict between England and Scotland, was, however, not subsiding. It was growing into a struggle that would become known as the First Scottish War of Independence. Since this book deals mostly with the exploits of the Scottish hero Robert the Bruce, we shall not delve deep into the causes and the details surrounding the broader Anglo-Scots conflict. Instead, we shall try and focus only on the role of Robert in that struggle. What we need to remember in this story is the bitter rivalry between the Bruce family and the Comyn family, the traditional Earls of Buchan. And since the Bruces sided with the English King, any clash between these two rival

Scottish families was a potential war between the two realms. Thus, it was in the end, perhaps the first strike in the war between England and Scotland was an attack on the Bruces. The attackers were, of course, the Comyns and their allies. On Easter Monday, March 26th, 1296, seven Scottish earls made a surprise attack on the Bruce-held Carlisle Castle. Of course, this was clearly seen as a Comyn attack on the Bruces. After the Bruces had to flee from Scotland to exile, Carlisle was their primary stronghold. Needless to say, the English King responded to this attack - and to Scotland's alliance with England's enemy, France - by an invasion. At the end of March 1296, his armies devastated the border city of Berwick, inflicting great casualties and destruction. In that same year occurred the Battle of Dunbar, the only significant clash of that early English campaign. It was a decisive English victory, which completely crushed Scotland's resistance. The English campaign was swift, decisive, and utterly brutal. As a result, King John Balliol was deposed by the same man who placed him at that position, King Edward I. Balliol was imprisoned at the Tower of London and became derisively known in Scotland as "Toom Tabard". The country was now governed by the English. Of course, this meant good news for the Bruces. Robert the Bruce and his father were now back in the possession of their ancestral holdings, Annandale and Carrick. It was an elaborate power play between wealthy and powerful noble houses, with the fate of entire kingdoms at stake for their own success and survival. Both the Bruces and the Comyns would stop at nothing to ensure their respective successes.

Historic sources tell us that in August 1296, Robert the Bruce and his father were both present at Berwick - together with more than 1,500 influential Scots - to swear fealty to the victorious King Edward I of England. Whole of the Lowlands were now effectively occupied by the English, and Edward would be known to posterity as "*Malleus Scotorum*", or "Hammer of the Scots".

Chapter IV

Roberts the Bruce's allegiance to the English King was never destined to last. After all, blood is blood, and its call can never be stifled or ignored. Their despotic rule over Scotland and their endless pretensions on this struggling realm could not be ignored by the oppressed nobles and clans. In July 1297 a rebellion broke out against King Edward I and the English. It was led by James Stewart, High Steward of Scotland, together with some influential figures such as the Bishop of Glasgow - Robert Wishart, the Earl of Fife - MacDuff, and young Robert the Bruce, also. At this point we can try and piece together the motives and beliefs of young Robert. Up to that point he was likely under the lead of his father, the Lord of Annandale. But now, rising against the English, he was likely acting of his own free will. Scholars agree that Robert the Bruce was likely inspired by his friends and allies, old friends and supporters of his grandfather's, and that he too felt the overwhelming current of Scottish patriotism that swept through the oppressed nation. After all, Robert the Bruce was Scottish most of all, and he could not ignore that call of blood. Interestingly, his father was not part of this new rebellion. It was clearly a time to choose sides, and Robert the Bruce - as we will see later - chose the right one.

Contemporary accounts by historians and chroniclers memorized for posterity a famous quote by Robert the Bruce, who was at that point an enthusiastic, confident, and inspiring noble knight. Joining the Scottish revolt, he traveled to his ancestral home at Annandale, gathering knights and supporters and calling his banners. Walter of Guisborough, a medieval English chronicler, writes that he addressed his noble followers thus:

"No man holds his own flesh and blood in hatred, and I am no exception. I must join my own people and the nation in which I was born. I ask that you please come with me, and you will be my councilors and close comrades."

Soon enough, it was apparent that young Robert the Bruce was one of the foremost patriotic nobles supporting the revolt against the English. Surviving documents show that he received several letters that ordered him to urgently support John de Warenne, Earl of Surrey, the foremost English military commander. Bruce outright refused and continued to be a foremost supporter of the Scottish cause. His importance in this cause is indicated by a surviving letter exchanged between the English King Edward and his subordinate, Hugh Cressingham. The latter expresses his opinion, writing: *"if you had the earl of Carrick (Robert the Bruce), the Steward of Scotland and his brother...you would think your business done".*

Around this time, two major battles of the First War of Scottish Independence occurred, but Robert the Bruce was not present in either one of them. The first was the Battle of Stirling Bridge, fought on September 11th, 1297. A stunning Scottish victory, it was led by Sir William Wallace, who would later be remembered as a true hero of Scotland. The second battle was fought on July 22nd, 1298 - the Battle of Falkirk. This time, however, the luck of Wallace had run out, and his forces suffered a big defeat. In this battle, MacDuff of Fife died, as did John Stewart. The historical chronicles of this period are rather confusing on the involvement of Robert the Bruce in the battles. What we know for certain is the fact that King Edward, upon his return to England after the major victory at Falkirk, assigned to his lead followers the "Lordships and Lands". However, the possessions of Robert the Bruce were excepted from these lists - for what reason it remains unknown. Oddly enough, further confusion arises with writings of the famed John of Fordun. He records that Robert the Bruce fought for the English at the Battle of Falkirk, serving under the Bishop of Durham, Annandale and Carrick, Anthony Bek. This claim has been highly disputed by modern historians. Not a single member of the Bruce family appears on the "Falkirk roll of arms", which lists out nobles present at the battle. Furthermore, we know that Robert the Bruce chose to lay waste on his possessions at Annandale, devastating Ayr Castle in order to prevent the English from garrisoning it and using it to their advantage. This fact alone tells us that he was still firmly rooted to the Scottish cause.

When Scottish morale largely collapsed after the defeat at Falkirk, William Wallace resigned his post as the Guardian of Scotland, the position established because of the lack of a monarch. It was now appointed to two men, who would act as joint Guardians. However, these two men were bitter rivals: they were Robert the Bruce and John "The Red" Comyn of Badenoch. The two men could not work together whatsoever: both had a fierce claim to the Scottish throne and considered one another as enemies. In order for some balance to be established in this dual guardianship, and the tensions to be lowered, a third Guardian was appointed in 1299, this being William Lamberton, the Bishop of St. Andrews. However, the situation did not appease Robert the Bruce, and he promptly resigned from the position in 1300, being replaced by the Earl of Angus instead. However, the rest of the guardians soon were replaced since most of them belonged to the Comyn "faction" of supporters. This resulted in a sole Guardian of Scotland being appointed, Sir John de Soules.

By summer 1301, the English King Edward I renewed his campaigns in Scotland. Bothwell and Turnberry were captured in the initial stages, but the Scots were proving to be a formidable enemy. The next year the two sides agreed to a truce. We learn that it was at this time that Robert the Bruce submitted to King Edward alongside other Scottish nobles, especially with rumors of John Balliol returning to the throne. Around this time, we see mention of Robert the Bruce in a curious letter dated from March 1302. In it, Robert addresses the monks of Melrose Abbey offering his formal apology. The reason for it is his unjust calling of the tenants of the monks into service in his army. In the letter, Robert the Bruce pledges that from that point on, he would "never again" require the monks to serve in the army unless it was a *"common army of the whole realm"*. From this letter we can perhaps start to recognize the patriotic leader role of Robert the Bruce that he would later fully flesh out in his role as King of Scots.

The conflict with England, however, did not wane. By 1303, Edward the Hammer of the Scots was once more on campaign, this time reaching Edinburgh and marching onto Perth. By August of that year, he was in Aberdeen, having marched across Dundee, Brechin, and Montrose. Triumphantly he marched through this land, now moving backwards towards Dunfermline, submitting the whole of the realm under his rule. Thus, he gave the nobles of Scotland no choice but to surrender. They did so in February 1304 - all of them except the noble hero William Wallace. However, there was no doubt that most of these nobles submitted against their will, and that the patriotic urges were still strong within many of them. Robert the Bruce, of course, was still a leading patriot. In June of 1304, he and William Lamberton, the Bishop of St. Andrews and the great campaigner for Scottish independence, signed a pact that "bound them to each other", in "friendship and alliance against all men". Scholars agree that this pact - still somewhat enigmatic

- is a sign of their unyielding patriotism. It was signed after both men heard of the tragic exploits of their countrymen besieged at Stirling Castle. Its defenders would not submit to the English King, who proceeded to bombard them into submission with his novel weapon, the "Warwolf", the largest trebuchet ever made. At this point, it becomes clear to historians that Robert the Bruce only maintained outward fealty to the English King. Inwardly, he was looking forward to his own ambitions within Scotland and was - undoubtedly - also fueled by a degree of patriotism. Both he and Lamberton made plans to stall as much as possible, awaiting the inevitable death of the English King, who was at that point an elderly man.

Around this time, the English authorities finally managed to capture the hero of the Scots who evaded them for so long. William Wallace was captured at Robroyston in 1305 and taken to London. There, he died a true martyr's death: the English had him dragged behind his horse, then emasculated, eviscerated, his bowels burned before him, and finally hanged, drawn, and quartered. His dismembered limbs had been displayed in Berwick, Stirling, Newcastle, and Perth, while his head, dipped in tar, was placed on the London Bridge. There is no doubt that the death of William Wallace - a true Scottish patriot - had a tremendous effect on Robert the Bruce and other patriotic Scottish nobles, and that it only deepened their wish to fight for the independence of their realm.

Chapter V

By late 1305, things were escalating to a whole new level and Robert the Bruce was stepping up to the true forefront of the political events. By that time, he was not only the Earl of Carrick, but also the 7th Lord of Annandale, his father having died the year before. This meant that he was now a powerful noble in his own right - having vast estates, castles, and incomes across the realm. His family was large too, and he was the "face" of the ancient Bruce family. Of course, he also had a very strong claim to the Scottish throne that could not be disputed. It was a lot of pressure and a lot to uphold, but Robert the Bruce was up to the task. In September of 1305, he was ordered by King Edward - by that time 66 years old - to place his castle at Kildrummy "in the keeping of such a man as he himself will be willing to answer for". This statement largely indicated that Edward mistrusted Robert, and that he "saw through" his superficial submission to the English. One person to blame for this mistrust of Edward's is none other but Bruce's chief rival, John Comyn of Badenoch. The ambitions of Robert the Bruce were cut short by the equally strong ambitions of the Comyn family, whose support lay in the claim of John Balliol - through whom they could get richer and stronger. Furthermore, John Comyn of Badenoch was arguably the most powerful noble in the whole of Scotland, holding immense estates, earldoms, lordships, and sheriffdoms. He was also the nephew of John Balliol, and also had a claim to the throne of his own - both from his paternal and his maternal sides.

In 1305, it became obvious that the secret pact that Bruce and Lamberton had signed was not so secret after all, and that rumors of it reached the English King. Aware of this, Robert the Bruce decided it was nigh time to settle his differences and enmity with John Comyn - for the benefit of the whole of Scotland. To that end, the two met at a conference in which Bruce suggested that the two men should settle their differences and "enter into agreement with each other". This, according to Robert the Bruce, would help both of them to restore the privileges they lost under the English, and to benefit all Scots and their rights. This agreement suggested that Comyn would support Bruce's claim to the throne, in exchange for the latter's entire lands - or vice versa: Bruce supporting Comyn's claim for his lands in compensation. Some chronicles and historians write that such a secret agreement was actually sworn, signed, and sealed in 1305, whereupon John Comyn of Badenoch actually agreed to abandon his claim to the Scottish throne in favor of Robert Bruce - if an uprising led by the latter would occur. In exchange he would receive the Bruce family lands. However, John Comyn most likely betrayed Robert the Bruce's intentions to King Edward - for his own gains. He did so in order to finally put an end to his chief rival. Robert the Bruce was at the English court at the moment and got a warning that he was betrayed and would be arrested. Ralph de Monthermer was the one to warn him, sending a cryptic message of "12 pence and a spur", which Robert understood was a sign for him to flee. He promptly fled back to Scotland.

Robert the Bruce arrived at Dumfries and met John Comyn of Badenoch for a private meeting on February 10th, 1306, at the Greyfriars Church. There Robert voiced his anger and reproached John for his base treachery, the latter denying the claims. In the ensuing argument, Robert the Bruce took out his dagger and stabbed John - without killing him. Robert ran out of the church and said to his attendants what was done. These two men, Roger de Kirkpatrick of Closeburn and Sir Robert Fleming, rushed back in to finish the deed and finally eliminate John Comyn. They stabbed him with swords and killed him. Comyn's companion at the scene, Robert Comyn, rushed to his aid but was struck in the head by Sir Christopher Seton and killed on the spot.

Following this controversial event, many different versions of the story surfaced. Many tried to paint Robert the Bruce as a villain, having lured John Comyn of Badenoch to a church under the pretense of a safe meeting (a church was seen as a holy place where blood was not to be shed), and then killing him in what seemed to be a premediated murder. Others attempted to find excuses for the killing, saying that it was done in the heat of the argument and fueled by the betrayal of John. Other sources say that Robert the Bruce was urged to slay Comyn once and for all by Sir Richard Edgar. Either way, we might never know the truth behind this secretive and crucial event. There is no doubt that Comyn had every reason to betray Robert the Bruce - and that the latter's reaction was dominated by anger and fiery emotions. In the decades that followed, various chroniclers and historians gave their own versions of the event. Some said that the two men argued and came to blows after Robert's accusation of treachery. This scuffle is perhaps the reason why Robert did not kill Comyn outright, but only wounded him. The medieval chronicle of Scotichronicon tells us that Comyn survived Bruce's attack and was being treated, when the two of the aforementioned supporters of Robert entered the church and finished the job, killing him. Nevertheless, this event was critical for the fate of Scotland that was in the balance. The death of John Comyn of Badenoch was a critical point of no return, and Bruce knew that he had to act. With his chief rival out of the way, Robert the Bruce could fully focus on his own ambitions and the independence of Scotland. To achieve this latter goal, he pressed his claim to the throne and embarked on a campaign to free his nation of the English.

The killing of John Comyn of Badenoch was seen by many as a dishonorable act of sacrilege, as Bruce committed murder within the sanctity of the church. However, his pact with Lamberton vouched that he had the support of the Scottish Church, and that his path to kingship was now open. His first action was an attack on Dumfries Castle, held at the time by an English garrison. From there, he rushed to Glasgow, eager to assert his claim to the throne. There he met with one of his supporters and old friends, Bishop Robert Wishart. Instead of excommunicating him for his sacrilegious deed, Wishart absolved Robert the Bruce of his sins and urged the folk and the clergy to support him and his cause. Together, they traveled to Scone, the ancestral place where Scottish kings were traditionally crowned. Met there by Bishop Lamberton and many other prominent nobles and church officials, on Palm Sunday, March 25th, 1306, aged 32, Robert the Bruce was crowned King of Scots. The event was conducted with all the formality that befitted the crowning of a king. Royal robes and vestments, up to that point well hidden from the English, were now brought out to adorn Robert's person. His crowning was witnessed by many of the chief Scottish nobles, including the Earls of Mar, Lennox, Atholl, and Menteith. The great and ancient royal banner of the Scottish Kings was brought out and unfurled above the new King's throne. And thereafter, he became King Robert I of Scotland. It was less than seven weeks after he stained his blade with the blood of John Comyn.

The very next day, Isabella, the Countess of Buchan, arrived at Scone. She was the wife of John Comyn, the 3rd Earl of Buchan (a cousin of John Comyn of Badenoch that was murdered). She however, belonged to the MacDuff family, the traditional Earls of Fife. The MacDuff's held an ancestral tradition of being the only clan that can crown a king of Scotland, and that was the claim she pressed on that day. Her brother, the heir of the MacDuff clan, was Donnchadh IV, the then Earl of Fife, but he was merely a child and also a captive of the English. Robert the Bruce went ahead and respected the traditions of Scotland, and so held a second coronation, equally splendorous, whereupon Isabella the Countess of Buchan, representing the MacDuff Clan, placed the Crown of Kings upon his noble crown, again proclaiming him the new King of the Scots.

Chapter VI

Needless to say, Robert the Bruce's bold new move was not met well with the English. King Edward I was furious, and by the spring of 1306 he renewed his campaigns against the Scots, marching northwards. Almost at once he proclaimed a new bill that excommunicated Robert the Bruce. His lands and estates Edward gifted to his own followers and loyal supporters. Furthermore, in his anger, Edward established a no mercy policy, ordering his troops and commanders that all Scots seized bearing arms, were to be executed without trial. As his most seasoned commander, Aymer de Valence, the Earl of Pembroke, was named the special lieutenant for Scotland.

Soon after, the two forces came to blows. King Robert the Bruce was likely unaware of Edward's new harsh policies of no mercy. Because of this, he followed the classic chivalric tradition of the medieval times and approached the garrisoned army of Valence in Perth. He personally called on Aymer de Valence to come out of the castle walls and do battle. Considered an honorable man, Valence offered an excuse of it being too late in the day. He claimed that he would accept the challenge to battle on the following day. Robert the Bruce accepted and placed his army to some nearby high-grounds, where they set up camp and disarmed. However, Aymer de Valence ignored the codes of chivalry and honor: when dark fell upon the land, he rode out of Perth with his army and descended upon the army of Robert the Bruce in a horrific surprise attack. This was the Battle of Methven, fought on June 19th, 1306. It was a catastrophic defeat for the Scots, and an early setback for the reign of King Robert the Bruce. Valence conducted a dishonorable attack, utterly decimating the Scottish army, outnumbering it as well. Historians note that Robert the Bruce fought valiantly in this clash: he was unhorsed three times, and three times he got back into the saddle, laying waste to his enemies. Alas, all efforts were in vain: he and his closest noble followers had to break out and flee, leaving many of the key Scottish nobles dead on the battlefield. Amongst those who had been captured or killed were David de Inchmartin, Hugh de la Haye, Alexander Scrymgeour (the Royal standard bearer), and many others. Initially, Aymer de Valence did not carry out the orders of King Edward, and refused to summarily execute these captive nobles. However, Edward had them hanged soon after. It was one of the major early losses of Scottish nobility in the First War of Scottish Independence. But not only did Robert the Bruce lose his close allies, but his family members as well. Soon after the battle, King Edward I captured three of his brothers, his daughter, his sisters, and his wife. The three brothers were soon after hanged, drawn, and quartered - a catastrophic and shocking loss for Robert the Bruce. The women were held in captivity in the harshest of conditions, some of them being displayed to the public in crude hanging cages.

Following his defeat at Methven, King Robert the Bruce was forced to flee into exile. Scholars today are uncertain where he was hiding at this time, spending the winter of 1306 and 1307 in seclusion. Some propose that he fled to Ireland or the Orkney Islands, while others propose that he found refuge in the Hebrides, at the estates of his close relatives, the Mar family. When the dust had settled however, Robert the Bruce decided to return to the Scottish mainland and continue the fight. He and his group of followers abandoned their exile in early 1307, in two groups. King Robert the Bruce arrived in February at his ancestral seat of Turnberry Castle, from where he began a guerrilla war against the English in southwest Scotland. The Scots again rushed to his side, flocking around their leader determined to rid themselves of English occupation. Soon enough, Robert struck back and won a small victory in the Battle of Glen Trool in April of 1307. The glens of Trool were a rough area, hard to traverse and even harder to fight in. Nevertheless, Robert the Bruce used his cunning to outmaneuver and defeat the English troops. The latter were forced to proceed in single file formation through the glen and were decimated by the Scots who ambushed them and dropped boulders from above. Many of the details about this battle are lost to history, but plenty of evidence suggests that it was a considerable achievement for Bruce at the time and that it undoubtedly served to boost the shaken Scottish morale. Furthermore, many historians and contemporary accounts termed this defeat as a major humiliation for the seasoned Earl of Pembroke, Aymer de Valence.

Following his win at Glen Trool, King Robert the Bruce continued his movements through the moors, by Dalmellington to Muirkirk, eventually emerging in the north of Ayrshire by early May 1307. There, he boosted his army with fresh and eager recruits. Around this time, he encountered the forces of Aymer de Valence once more. A clash between the two armies was once more inevitable, and Robert the Bruce took up a position on May 10th, placing his army on a plain close to Loudoun Hill. This plain was some 500 yards wide and bordered on both sides by deep morasses. That way, he ensured that his army could not be outflanked so easily by the enemy. Another account tells us that Robert prepared for the coming battle by digging three deep ditches in front of his troops - a serious obstacle for any attacker. What ensued was the fateful Battle of Loudoun Hill, fought on May 10th, 1307. Historian John Barbour mentions these events in his interesting, rhymed account:
"The king upon the other side,

Whose prudence was his valour's guide,
Rode out to see and chose his ground.
The highway took its course, he found,
Upon a medow, smooth and dry.
But close on either side therby
A bog extended, deep and broad,
That from the highway, where men rode,
Was full a bowshot either side.
He had three deep ditches made there
For if he could not well prevail at meeting them at the first,
He would have the second under his control,
Or finally the third.
The king's men met them at the dyke
So stoutly that the most warlike
And strongest of them fell to the ground.
Then could be heard a dreadful sound
As spears on armor rudely shattered,
And cries and groans the wounded uttered.
For those that first engaged in fight
Battled and fought with all their might.
Their shouts and cries rose loud and clear;
A grievous noise it was to hear."

It was now obvious that King Robert the Bruce was a shrewd tactician, and that his choice of battle positions was more than favorable. One major disadvantage for the English commander, Aymer de Valence, was the fact that he had to approach the Scots over a "highway" that stretched through a bog. Not only was this ground unfavorable, but his room for adequate deployment of troops was seriously limited because of parallel ditches that the Scots prepared. Any numerical superiority that the English had was rendered ineffective because of these obstacles. The only approach of attack that Valence had remaining was along a narrow and constricted front, which led his troops directly onto the waiting Scottish spears. In many ways, Loudoun Hill was reminiscent of an earlier Scottish triumph - the Battle of Stirling Bridge, where the English were likewise "funelled" towards the awaiting Scots.

Loudoun Hill was a place where King Robert the Bruce shined: he won a decisive and commendable victory over the English, inflicting heavy casualties. He faced the 3,000-strong English army with just 600 Scottish troops, and still emerged victorious. Hundreds and hundreds of English troops were left dead on the battlefield. It was the first major military victory of Robert the Bruce, and forever remained as one of his best early achievements.

Around the time of this battle, James Douglas also made his first actions, fighting for his King, Robert the Bruce. He made actions in southwest Scotland, notably by attacking and burning his own castle of Douglasdale. It was a major sign that Scotland as a whole was arising in revolt, with Bruce at its helm.

Bruce continued his movements, seeking to capitalize on his victory at Loudoun Hill. He captured Urquhart and Inverlochy Castles, devastated Nairn and Inverness Castle, and threatened Elgin as well.

Around this time, another major event transpired - one that was eagerly awaited by all Scots, Bruce in particular. That event was the death of English King Edward I, the Hammer of the Scots. He died on July 7th, 1307, having contracted dysentery while moving northwards into Scotland to confront Bruce. Sick, his health rapidly deteriorating, Edward camped his army near Carlisle on July 6th. He was dead the following morning. It was his son who became King of England at that point - Edward II of Caernarfon. And he would promptly continue his efforts against the Scottish King.

Chapter VII

The war for Scotland's freedom continued in earnest, and Loudoun Hill was the wind that gave speed to the freedom fighters. In late 1307, Robert the Bruce shifted his operations to the area of Aberdeenshire and was near Banff before becoming ill. It is likely that he was too worn out with the heavy campaigning and the hardships of military life, and it took a toll on his health. Sources state that during this period, Robert had to be carried everywhere by his loyal supporters. The conflict with the Comyns still persisted however, as they were chief English allies and by that point the hated rivals of the Bruces. During Robert's brief illness, John Comyn, the 3rd Earl of Buchan, remained at large in the King's rear. However, Bruce recovered rather speedily, and promptly returned to action. He marched his troops to the west, taking Duffus and Balvenie Castles, and then on to Black Isle where he captured Tarradale Castle in 1308. Following these achievements, he swung back across Inverness and towards Elgin, after which occurred the Battle of Inverurie, fought on May 23rd, 1308. In this clash, Bruce finally dealt with his foremost domestic enemy, John Comyn, the Earl of Buchan.

Not much of this campaign is known to us today, as no significant information survived through time. Nevertheless, we know with certainty that Bruce marched into the traditional Buchan lands held by the Comyns, and a clash soon became a looming threat. Comyn attempted an attack at one point, near Slioch, but was repulsed and no significant battle occurred. Next, in May 1308, Robert the Bruce reached the outskirts of Inverurie and made camp on its far side. The Earl of Buchan gathered his forces for battle.

It is said that the Buchan army morale was exceptionally high, in part because Robert the Bruce was still ill. John Comyn knew this, and spread the word amongst his troops, saying that the enemy commander could not take the field. Such was the reputation of Robert the Bruce. However, the King found enough strength and composure, rising from his sick bed and taking the control of his armies in the field. It is said that the Buchan army morale suddenly plummeted, after the raw feudal recruits spotted King Robert the Bruce in the field, in all his glory. Again, John Barbour left to posterity one of his rhyming accounts, and much about the Battle of Inverurie can be gathered from it.

> *"The king came on in fine array*
> *With much display his foes stood set*
> *Until the ranks were nerly met.*
> *But when his foemen saw the king*
> *Advancing without lingering,*
> *A little on their reins they drew.*
> *The king by this time right well knew*
> *That in their hearts they were distressed,*
> *And with his banners forward pressed.*
> *Thus they retreated more and more.*
> *And when the small folk with them saw*
> *Their leaders all retreating so,*
> *They quickly turned their backs to go,*
> *And fled and scattered far and wide.*
> *Their lords, that still were side by side,*
> *When they beheld the small folk flee,*
> *And the king advancing steadily,*
> *Themselves became disheartened so*
> *That they, too, turned their backs to go.*

A short while stayed they side by side,
And then they scattered far and wide."

Early on, Bruce's army was bruised by a surprise attack by Comyn archers. However, still-ill Robert rose up to the task and managed to counter-attack, facing the Comyn army head on. From all accounts, it is likely that he recognized the critical moment in the battle, when the enemy morale wavered, and then pressed on with full force. Soon enough, all enemy lines broke into panic, and began fleeing. Seeing that the troops could not be gathered, John Comyn, the 3rd Earl of Buchan - fled as well. The Battle of Inverurie was a decisive victory for Robert the Bruce, and it finally subdued his chief domestic opponents, the Comyns. What followed after this battle was a grim episode in the reign of Robert the Bruce. In order to make sure that the historic lands of the Comyns would not remain an active threat at his rear, Robert the Bruce ordered these lands to be sacked and plundered in full. What ensued is known today as the Harrying of Buchan, or Rape of Buchan. He ordered his brother, Edward de Bruce, to harry, destroy, and pillage the entirety of Buchan - from one end to the other. This included fields, farms, villages, castles, livestock, and all of value and function. Edward proceeded with the task, and for several months he laid waste to these bountiful lands. In the process, he inflicted immense damage with utmost ruthlessness. Many civilians undoubtedly died, livestock was slaughtered en-masse, houses burned, grain and food stores destroyed, earth scorched. It was a violent reprisal against the Comyns and their allies and was perhaps the quickest way for Robert the Bruce to ensure that no one ever again would stand up against his rule in this part of Scotland. And so it was, never again did the people of Buchan stand up against Bruce's rule. What is more, the harrying had such a profound effect on them, that they never again had any loyalties for the Comyn clan. With this violent episode, Robert the Bruce effectively destroyed the power base of the Comyn Clan. Without a doubt it was an ugly affair - but it served its purpose. And it was a major achievement: the Comyns held power in northeast Scotland for more than a century. In just a month of violence and devastation, Bruce reduced that power to nothing. John Comyn, the 3rd Earl of Buchan fled to England, where he died the following year. His death and the rape of Buchan together created a major power shift in medieval Scotland.

Following the rape of Buchan, Robert turned his focus towards the English garrisons at Aberdeen Castle. In late 1308 he laid siege to the castle and quickly won, destroying it in the process. Many historians and scholars are having a tough time understanding just how Robert the Bruce managed to subdue so many castles in such a short amount of time. It is true that much of the hard historical facts about this period simply do not exist, but those that we know with certainty still create a bit of a conundrum. We know that Bruce's army at the time was not exceptionally large, and he certainly did not have siege weapons. The size of his army allowed him to move throughout the highlands with relative speed, but tackling castles was a different thing altogether. Some scholars suggest that the extremely low morale of the Comyns and their allies had a significant role to play in Robert's success. This, and the vicious harrying of Buchan, could have left them unwilling and unable to oppose King Robert the Bruce in any major way.

Less threatening enemies still remained, however. Amongst the foremost Comyn supporters was the MacDougall Clan. The greatest stronghold of this clan was their Dunstaffnage Castle, where the last of the Comyn supporters were holed up. Robert the Bruce now shifted his focus on the MacDougalls, having finished with Buchan.

The chief of the MacDougall Clan, Alexander, was too old and frail to actively participate in fighting against Bruce. It was his son and heir who led the conflict, John Bacach ("the Lame"). By all surviving historic accounts, Bacach led his clan army and took up defensive positions around the narrow Pass of Brander in Lorne. He placed his men in an ambush position, hiding them in the woods from where they were ready to descend upon Bruce if he would pass there. However, it was not enough to trick King Robert: by that point he was well aware of the guerilla style of clan warfare, having done it himself. He saw through the MacDougall plan and decided to take a different approach. He sent his chief commander, Sir James "the Black" Douglas, with a contingent of archers, to take a different route and place themselves - unobserved - at the enemy's rear. When the battle finally erupted, with the MacDougalls attacking, Both Robert and Black Douglas sprang into action. They crushed the MacDougall army in a vice-like attack. The enemy panicked and fled, and the MacDougall leaders ended up in exile in England, just like the Earl of Buchan. There is evidence that suggests that Robert the Bruce conducted further harryings, just like in Buchan, this time in Argyll and Bute in the MacDougall lands. However, it seems that the devastation was not as great as before. Either way, there remained a lot of resentment for Robert the Bruce in these parts of Scotland.

Chapter VIII

Following these events, King Robert the Bruce continued his steady course of action in Scotland. By March 1309, he held his first parliament in St. Andrews, and by August that year he had control over all of Scotland north of River Tay. Ever since the murder of John "the Red" Comyn and his crowning, Robert the Bruce had the full support of the Scottish Church, even though he was officially excommunicated by the Pope. This support of the Scottish clergy was a particularly crucial factor in Robert's rise to kingship and his subsequent successes. In 1310, the Scottish clergy formally recognized him as the King at a general council. We know that on October 1st, 1310, Robert wrote to the English King Edward II, in an attempt to establish peace between the two realms. The attempt was unsuccessful. To that end, Robert continued to fight against the English garrisons in Scotland, freeing numerous castles over the next three years. In 1310 he took Linlithgow, Dumbarton in 1311, and Perth in 1312. Interestingly, he also raided northern England, but more importantly the Isle of Man. In mid-1313 he landed at Ramsey and laid siege to Castletown's Castle Rushen. This he captured and thus denied the English the use of this important strategic island. In fact, Castle Rushen was captured by Robert the Bruce three times. For years, King Robert led a highly efficient guerilla war against the English, refusing deliberately to meet them in open battle and on even ground. Historians called him one of the greatest guerilla leaders of all time. The style was exhausting but highly efficient and allowed him to systematically free parts of Scotland and reduce the English garrisons. And if we consider the fact that Robert was raised as a classic medieval feudal knight, this fact comes as a bit of a surprise. It certainly differed from what Robert was taught as a young man. Either way, he found himself perfectly up to the task. By 1314, he actually retook most of the castles in Scotland that were occupied by the English and could actually raid the north of England as far as Carlisle. This, of course, would not go unpunished by the English: Edward II was ready to mount a major military expedition into Scotland. For this reason, he assembled a vast army that numbered between 15,000 and 20,000 men. By spring of 1314, Robert the Bruce was focused on Stirling Castle however, one of the most important and formidable fortifications in the whole of Scotland. Its English governor, Philip de Mowbray, held out fervently, but agreed to surrender to Bruce if he was not relieved by June 24th, 1314. Bruce's commanders were also in action: Black Douglas went on to capture Roxburgh, while Thomas Randolph captured Edinburgh Castle. However, when Edward II heard the news of the besieged Stirling Castle, he decided to act. He embarked on a speeded march from the port town of Berwick, with the intention of relieving the besieged garrison. At the time, Robert's army numbered just around 5,500 and 6,500 troops, most of them spearmen. Nevertheless, he prepared to prevent the English from reaching Stirling Castle. What ensued was one of the most important battles in the history of Scotland, and certainly one of the foremost achievements of King Robert the Bruce. It was the Battle of Bannockburn, and it would etch his name into the pages of history.

The army that King Edward II sent into Scotland was by far the largest that invaded it up to that point. It was, without a doubt, the clear proof of Edward's intent: to once and for all subdue Scotland and deal with Robert the Bruce. We know from surviving documents that Edward II requested around 2,000 heavy cavalry and 25,000 infantry: substantial numbers for that time. However, it is unknown whether the entirety of that request was met, and if such numbers entered Scotland in 1314. Either way, it was an immense army and undoubtedly dwarfed whatever Robert the Bruce could muster. So, it was clear even before the battle that the Scots would be at a numerical disadvantage since they numbered no more than 6,000 infantry and around 500 cavalry. As an added disadvantage, the Scots were not equipped as properly as the Englishmen. The majority of the Scottish troops were spearmen, with others wielding axes, pikes, and some swords in between. However, such an army was perfect for light skirmishing or guerilla warfare, which Bruce often employed in his campaigns. Still, being positioned close to Stirling, Bruce was in no position for guerilla tactics, and it would come down to the basics when the enemy arrived. The Battle of Bannockburn was fought on June 23rd and 24th, 1314. However, on the 23rd, the two armies were separated by eight miles, and it was uncertain whether the two parties would ever meet. And it was exactly this delay that Robert the Bruce would take advantage of and strategically place his army to the west, in a place with plenty of hillocks. In the meantime, Edward II decided to conduct a challenging, rapid march, covering around 70 miles in just a single week. This left his troops weary and hungry. Historians of modern times are severely critical of this move.

Nevertheless, the English army began preparations for battle once they arrived near Stirling. Edward II of Caernarfon was perhaps somewhat limited in his battle experience at the time, but he still had a good array of close advisors, many of whom were seasoned battle commanders. Together, they agreed that Robert the Bruce was likely to place his troops in boggy grounds, which Edward reckoned were near the River Forth, close to Stirling. Orders were sent to the troops for such positioning. Soon enough, the English army was on the move, and it is likely that they moved in four divisions. What we know from history is that Robert the Bruce arrayed his troops in special defensive formations, known as "schiltrons." We know of these formations from our previous books related to the Scottish Middle Ages, as the "schiltron" was widely used throughout. A bit aged in 1314, perhaps, this formation hailed likely from the Viking era and the shield walls of that time. But still, they could be a formidable formation especially for those defending from an enemy charge. Let us remind ourselves that the "schiltron" is a strong defensive square made up of pikemen. Once assembled, this square bristles with pikes which can be quite hard to penetrate.

The command of the Scottish vanguard (forward attacking positions) was given to Thomas Randolph, the 1st Earl of Moray and a close ally of Robert the Bruce. Leading the vanguard was a place of honor, awarded only to the bravest and most deserving allies. Robert himself commanded the rearguard, while the third part of the army was led by his brother, Edward. Also present was the famed James "Black" Douglas, commanding an additional, fourth, division of the army. On June 23rd, the battle that would resound in history finally began. However, it did not start in earnest, but rather as some light skirmishing. The English army attempted to push across the high grounds of the Bannock Burn (from where the battle gets its name), an area surrounded by marshlands. Around this time, a crucial event was witnessed by all present: the death of the English knight, Sir Henry de Bohun. This young warrior was the grandson of the English Earl of Hereford, and - by all accounts - an enthusiastic and confident knight. During the skirmishing, he spotted King Robert the Bruce, astride a small and light palfrey (type of horse). Without a doubt, the youth thought that he was such an able warrior that he could take on Bruce in single combat and kill him, thus ending the battle quickly and acquiring immense fame. However, he overestimated his abilities incredibly. Fully armored in knightly fashion, Henry de Bohun lowered his great lance and being now spotted by Bruce, charged at full speed at the Scottish King. Of course, such a charge from a heavily armed and armored knight - if successful - was devastating and certainly fatal. But Robert the Bruce was ready: he stood calmly, letting Bohun charge at him. In a critical moment, in the fragment of a second, he lightly moved his horse out of the way, avoided the great war lance by a fraction, rose up in his saddle and landed a devastating blow with his battle axe. This blow was so fierce that it split Bohun's helmet and skull clear in half, shattering the ax in the process. Calm and composed, Robert the Bruce nonchalantly regretted the splitting of his favorite weapon. This magnificent case of single combat was well witnessed by all, and greatly influenced Bruce's fearsome reputation. After this event, the English withdrew for the rest of the day, the battle far from over.

On the next day, June 24th, the Battle of Bannockburn continued, with the English continuing to advance, confident in their superior numbers. As they emerged from a wooded area of New Park, the English sighted the full array of the Scottish army, much to their surprise. Edward and his battle planners wrongly judged the intentions of the Scots and found them at the place they did not expect. Because of this surprise, the English kept their forces in marching order, and not arrayed in battle positions as usual. Their cavalry, the most potent of their weapons, was now constricted by the odd terrain and could not maneuver properly. The Scots faced them with a majority of spearmen. In normal circumstances, the English would have placed archers to the front, and rain arrows upon the spearmen, breaking them up. Now, however, their archers were at the back, giving them further disadvantage. Robert the Bruce cunningly placed his army where *he* wanted, creating a pitched battle in his favor - allowing him to await the English completely prepared.

As a result, the Battle of Bannockburn was a terrifying loss for the English. The spears of the Scottish schiltrons pummeled and decimated the English cavalry, while the infantry - whose morale was already low - was utterly devastated. It was a marvelous victory of Robert the Bruce, and one that cemented his reputation as an able warrior. English troops soon broke and fled, leaving many casualties on the ground. Sources state that as much as 11,000 English infantrymen died in this battle, and the defeat was dubbed a "calamity of stunning proportions" for the English. Amongst the dead and captured were many nobles of great importance. Those noble Englishmen who died were, amongst others: William Marshal, Marshal of Ireland; Gilbert de Clare, 8th Earl of Gloucester; John Comyn, Lord of Badenoch (son of the murdered John "the Red" Comyn); John de Montfort, 2nd Baron Montfort; Robert de Clifford, 1st Baron de Clifford; Edmund Hastings, 1st Baron Hastings; and many, many more. Many more notable nobles were captured. King Edward II fled the battle in the most critical moment, escaping capture or death by mere moments. He was led away by his two guards, Aymer de Valence and Sir Giles d'Argentan and 500 royal bodyguards. Sir Giles d'Argentan had the reputation of being an incredibly powerful warrior, perhaps the third-best knight in all of Europe. Once they were clear of the danger, he boldly announced to King Edward II: *"Sire, your protection was committed to me, but since you are safely on your way, I will bid you farewell for never yet have I fled from a battle, nor will I now."* He turned his horse, charged back into the thick of the Scottish ranks, where he died in battle. Edward II soon fled to Berwick and then to York in England. Robert the Bruce quickly captured the Stirling Castle he was besieging. The

Battle of Bannockburn was one of the foremost victories in the life of Robert the Bruce and served to pave the way towards the recognition of Scotland's hard-earned independence.

After this Scottish victory, much had changed for Robert the Bruce. He now had the freedom to raid the north of England, launching expeditions as far as Yorkshire and Lancashire. But more importantly, Robert the Bruce felt bold enough to expand his war against the English by launching an expedition into Ireland, in an attempt to conquer it. This is known as the Bruce Campaign in Ireland, and it began in 1315. The military expedition was commanded by Robert's brother, Edward the Bruce. In a way, it was a way for two oppressed Gaelic nations to help one another: Scotland and Ireland. Bruce's intention was to assist the Irish nobles who lost lands to the English invaders, and to help them repel them. It was, however, also a way for Bruce to deal with the remaining members of the Balliol family and their supporters, who had fled to Ireland, most notably John MacDougall, known as John Bacach, whom Robert had already defeated before. Initially, Edward the Bruce had moderate success, conquering many areas of Ireland. However, by 1318, it was evident that he could not effectively hold all these areas and could not feed his army. As a result, he had to resort to pillaging, earning animosity from the folk, and his army was reduced in numbers. On October 14th, 1318, Edward the Bruce was defeated and killed in the Battle of Faughart, and his death effectively ended the Bruce expedition in Ireland.

Chapter IX

One of Robert's ideas that lay behind the invasion of Ireland was related to the shared cultural identity of the two nations. It was a peculiar ideology that is today called a "Pan-Gaelic Greater Scotia". It was a propaganda campaign with which Robert the Bruce attempted to unite the Gaels against the English. Of course, this would be done in favor of Scotland, and Bruce and his lineage would rule over both Ireland and Scotland. Of course, these were not just despotic pretensions on the realm of Ireland: Robert had valid connections to its royal lineage that he could use to justify this ideology. Notably, he had connections to the de Burgh family and the Earldom of Ulster through his marriage. But most importantly, he had connections through Carrick and his mother who descended from both Irish and Scottish Gaelic royalty. In fact, Robert the Bruce was a (somewhat distant) descendant of Aoife of Leinster and through her a descendant of Brian Boru and the Irish Kings of Leinster. In many of his letters of that time, Robert the Bruce stressed his royal lineage and equalized both Irish and Scots as Gaelic brethren with shared language and heritage, calling their planned union as "our nation." He wrote:

"Whereas we and you and our people and your people, free since ancient times, share the same national ancestry and are urged to come together more eagerly and joyfully in friendship by a common language and by common custom, we have sent you our beloved kinsman, the bearers of this letter, to negotiate with you in our name about permanently strengthening and maintaining inviolate the special friendship between us and you, so that with God's will our nation (nostra nacio) may be able to recover her ancient liberty."

Sadly, the Bruce invasion of Ireland came at a bad moment. The land was beset by hardships, experiencing a debilitating famine, and the poor folk of Ireland had a hard time seeing any differences between the English and Scottish invaders - since they suffered all the same. The idea of a Pan-Gaelic union was not executed well enough, which is a saddening fact all on its own, since such a union could have benefited both the Irish and the Scots in the long run.

As the King of Scots, Robert the Bruce was noted not just for his military accomplishments, but also for his many diplomatic achievements. One of the foremost of these is the 1320 Declaration of Arbroath, which was actually a letter sent to Pope John XXII. Signed by influential Scottish nobles, it addressed the matter of Robert's excommunication, and a clear assertion of Scotland's antiquity and independence, free from English rule. As a result, the Pope eventually removed the excommunication. It was a big step towards independence, and just eight years later, Robert the Bruce signed the Treaty of Edinburgh-Northampton together with the English King Edward III. This treaty effectively recognized Scotland as an independent kingdom, and Robert the Bruce as its rightful King. Through struggle and perseverance, Robert the Bruce led Scotland through its period of darkness and into a new age of freedom and independence. After a lengthy struggle with his rivals, he at last emerged on top and announced to the enemies of his kingdom that a new and able warrior was now defending it. Bannockburn was Robert's crown jewel, and from that bloodshed he carved out an independent Scotland.

Alas, fate would not grant Robert the Bruce, the King of Scots, a lengthy reign. Illness troubled him in the latter half of his rule, heralding an untimely end. From at least 1327, Robert suffered from some serious illness, as contemporary accounts and surviving documents tell us. What was this illness? We do not know for certain today. In medieval Scotland, medicine was in its infancy, and the healers had a rather narrow view and limited knowledge of the many ailments that could have troubled Robert. However, two chronicles of the era, Scalacronica and the Lanercost Chronicle, mention leprosy as the likely option. A French author of the time, Jean le Bel, mentions in 1327 that Robert suffered from "la grosse maladie", a contemporary name that often-denoted leprosy. Still, we need to keep in mind that medieval scholars used the term leprosy freely, often when leprosy was not the cause of illness. Either way, letters and documents from this time indicate that the illness struck Robert in episodes. For example, a letter dated July 1327 states that Robert the Bruce was so ill that "he can scarcely move anything but his tongue" and was bound to die. Others wrote that the King contracted his illness "through a benumbing brought on by his cold lying," i.e., from sleeping on ground during his exile and guerilla campaigns. It seems like a far-fetched idea. Still, we do not know for sure what caused Robert's serious health decline in the 1320s. Modern scholars suggest a variety of possible conditions, varying from syphilis, tuberculosis, cancer, or just a series of strokes.

Alas, all signs pointed to the sad fact that Robert the Bruce, the Hero of Scotland, was not to live for much longer. One of the last major events in his reign occurred in October 1328, when the Pope finally lifted the interdict from Scotland and canceled Robert's excommunication. Around this time, Robert the Bruce made what appears to have been his final journey. It was an apparent pilgrimage to Whithorn, the site of St. Ninian's shrine. It was here that the supposed first Christian church in Scotland was built in 397 AD. Perhaps Robert wanted to search for a cure to his illness there, or simply to "make his peace with God." En-route to Whithorn, he first sailed to the Isle of Arran, staying there for Christmas of 1328. From there he visited his ancestral home of Turnberry Castle, there to visit his son and his bride, and then traveled overland to Wigtownshire. Accounts state that he was too ill and had to be carried on a litter. It is likely that at this point his health deteriorated severely. Around March 1329 it is recorded that he stayed at Glenluce Abbey and at Monreith, and from there he visited the famed Cave of St. Ninian. In April of that year, he reached his destination, visiting the Whithorn Shrine of St. Ninian. Records tell us that he fasted and prayed for some five days, and then returned back to his manor at Cardross, traveling by sea. Back at his home, Robert began preparations for the "other life." To his bedside he summoned all his most chief nobles, so they could witness his many gifts to churches and monasteries, and donations to religious foundations. This was likely a way for Robert to perpetuate his memory for posterity, and to secure the salvation of his soul. During this period of the middle ages, most monarchs were deeply religious, especially on their deathbeds. He also expressed his deep regrets for not being able to embark on a Crusade to the Holy Land, there to fight "Saracens." As one of his final wishes, he wanted his heart to be removed after he die, and then to be taken on a pilgrimage to Jerusalem, to the Church of the Holy Sepulcher. Some other sources state that he simply wished for his heart to be "carried in battle against God's Foes." Chroniclers recorded his words:

"I will that as soone as I am trespassed out of this worlde that ye take my harte owte of my body, and embawme it, and take of my treasoure as ye shall thynke sufficient for that enterprise, both for your selfe and suche company as ye wyll take with you and present my harte to the holy Sepulchre whereas our Lorde laye, seyng my body can nat come there."

Chapter X

On June 7th, 1329, King Robert the Bruce died in his manor at Cardross. He was 54, one month shy of 55. The bringer of Scotland's freedom, the unsung hero of Alba, the formidable warrior of the British Isles - was cut in his prime by an illness that swiftly overtook him. His was a lifetime of struggle: from the feuds and goals of his grandfather, passed on to his father, and then picked up by him - all the way to the long-coveted independence of Scotland. He was gone before his time, but even so he made sure that all of his goals were fulfilled. And even after he died, his accomplishments continued: six days after his death special Papal bulls were issued, which granted the privilege of unction at the coronation ceremonies of all future Kings of Scots.

For many decades modern scholars have studied the surviving accounts in order to decipher the exact cause of Robert's death. It was certain that an illness claimed his life, him being just 54 at the time. And although contemporary sources mostly claimed leprosy as the cause of death, modern scholars firmly denounce this theory. As the King of Scots, Robert the Bruce could not possibly function in all his duties as a leper. Besides, all accounts state that he was not isolated in any way from others, indicating that his illness was not infectious - which leprosy *is*. In fact, later scientific research concluded that Robert did not have leprosy. This still left a question mark over the cause of his death, and many theories were placed forward. Some even suggested that it was his rich courtly diet that hastened his demise and contributed to the illness. A contemporary account from Robert's own physician, Maino de Maineri, criticizes Robert's habit of eating eels, calling it "dangerous to his health."

As per Robert's deathbed wishes, his body was embalmed, and his heart removed from his chest. The latter was also embalmed and placed in a special silver casket, which was designed to be worn around the neck. This casket was worn by Sir James "the Black" Douglas. Robert's viscera (removed during embalming) were interred in the Chapel of Saint Serf. Today, the ruins of this church are located in Dumbarton, in the picturesque Levengrove Park. The embalmed body of the King was transported to its burial place in a grandiose funereal ceremony. An incredible 3,040 kilograms (~6,700 lbs) of wax was purchased for the creation of funerary candles. It was, all in all, a very grand affair, as befitted such a grand King of Scots. A special carriage, draped in black mourning cloth, traveled eastwards towards Robert's final resting place at Dunfermline Abbey. Scotland's leading nobles and knights, in mourning, accompanied the King's hearse. At the abbey, Robert's body, laid in a wooden coffin was buried, with all royal ceremonies, within a special stone vault beneath the floor. Above was a box tomb made of luxurious white Italian marble. The whole monument was topped with a white alabaster effigy of Robert's - itself painted and gilded. A special inscription adorned the tomb:

"Hic jacet invictus Robertus Rex benedictus qui sua gesta legit repetit quot bella peregit ad libertatem perduxit per probitatem regnum scottorum: nunc vivat in arce polorum" ("Here lies the invincible blessed King Robert / Whoever reads about his feats will repeat the many battles he fought / By his integrity he guided to liberty the Kingdom of the Scots: May he now live in Heaven")

After the King was laid to rest, there still remained the question of fulfilling his last request - carrying his heart to Jerusalem. This task was given to one of the most formidable warriors of Robert's retinue - James "the Black" Douglas. However, an international crusade was never realized, and Douglas embarked on a quest that led him to Spain. It is likely that he simply wanted to carry Robert's heart into battle against Muslims, since a journey to Jerusalem was not possible, because the city was in Muslim hands since 1187. Hearing that the Spanish King, Alfonso XI of Castile, was planning a military campaign against the Muslim Moorish Kingdom of Granada, Sir James Douglas traveled there with a small retinue of noble knights and squires. Around August 1330, Douglas and the other Scots were part of the Spanish army that was besieging the castle of Teba. In the ensuing fighting, under circumstances that were never explained to this very day, Black Douglas and his retinue all died in combat. Many theories of their death exist, but none can be accepted with certainty. Some sources point out a "foreign count" (possibly Douglas), who perished in the battle because he acted rashly. It is possible that Douglas made a premature attack, or perhaps an attempt to rescue one of his party, and thus died fighting the Moors. One popular anecdote states that Douglas - seeing that his situation was dire - threw the heart of Robert the Bruce amongst the surrounding enemies and said: *"Now pass thou onward as thou wert wont, and Douglas will follow thee or die."* Thus, he symbolically followed Robert the Bruce into battle for one last time. The heart was, however, not lost. Accounts state that the surviving members of Douglas' retinue recovered both his dead body and the heart of Bruce, returning both of them to Scotland. The heart of Robert the Bruce - having fought one last time against "God's foes" - has been interred ceremoniously at Melrose Abbey in Roxburghshire.

Sadly, the grandeur of Robert's burial could not survive the turning wheel of time. The Dunfermline Abbey was victim to the tides of history and was sacked in 1560 during the turbulent period of the Scottish Reformation. Parts of it were roofless by 1563, and accounts from that period describe it in a ruinous state and a "danger to enter". Parts of it collapsed in 1672, and further elements collapsed in 1716. By late 1700s, the resting place of the legendary Robert the Bruce was a complete ruin. However, it was well known that Dunfermline Abbey stood on that site, and by 1818, a new church was planned to be raised there. During construction work, workmen discovered a vault. Within it was a decayed oak coffin, containing a body encased in a lead shroud. At the head, that shroud was shaped into a crown. Without a doubt, leading scholars of the time knew that it was the body of Robert the Bruce that they had discovered. In late 1819, a special investigation was begun in order to closely examine the remains of both the body and the luxurious alabaster remains. Once the lead casing was removed, a skeleton was examined by two leading Professors of Anatomy at the University of Edinburgh. One of the telltale proofs that it was, in fact, Robert the Bruce that they examined, was a sawn open sternum - from where his heart was removed. Afterwards, they made detailed measurements of the whole body and plaster casts of his skull, revealing that the King - in his prime - stood some 185 centimeters (6' 1"). For medieval standards, this would have been seen as truly impressive, and worthy of a king. On November 5th, 1819, King Robert the Bruce was once more ceremoniously interred into the vault at Dunfermline Abbey, his remains placed into a new lead coffin and preserved with 1,500 lbs of molten pitch.

The famed King of the Scots, Robert the Bruce, lives on in the hearts and memory of the Scottish nation. Much is owed to him by every Scot - their freedom and independence most of all. A man of iron determination, cunning, and perseverance, he fought the

English with stubbornness and passion that only an oppressed monarch could feel. Against all odds, outnumbered and underpowered, Robert the Bruce stood against the formidable and massive English army - and decimated it. One of the most renowned warriors of his generation, and certainly one of the best knights of the European middle ages, Robert the Bruce was unequaled in times before and after him. Today, his achievements and all his battles are a staple in every history book. From them, historians can learn so much and study in detail the emergence of an independent Scottish Kingdom. We too, can learn valuable lessons from the life and times of Robert the Bruce. We can learn that even against the odds, one can win and succeed. We can learn to stay true to our goals and dreams, and to follow them true to the last. And we can only hope and dream to be remembered across generations, as Robert the Bruce was.

References:

Brouwer, M. 2020. *Robert the Bruce and the Scottish Independence.* Radboud University.

Penman, M. 2005. *King Robert the Bruce (1274-1329).* Études Écossaises.

Penman, M. *Reputations in Scottish History: King Robert the Bruce (1274-1329).*

Penman, M. 2014. *Robert the Bruce: King of the Scots.* Yale University Press.

Pitcairn, S. and Johnston, W. T. *King Robert the Bruce.* Royal Dunfermline.

Scott, T. 1998. *Tales of King Robert the Bruce: Freely Adapted from The Brus of John Barbour (14th Century).* Gordon Wright.

Unknown. 2016. *Robert the Bruce and the Kildrum Letter.* Culture NL.

Don't miss out!

Visit the website below and you can sign up to receive emails whenever History Nerds publishes a new book. There's no charge and no obligation.

https://books2read.com/r/B-A-ODOK-RGSYB

BOOKS 2 READ

Connecting independent readers to independent writers.

Also by History Nerds

Celtic History
Ireland

Great Wars of the World
World War 1
World War 2
The Napoleonic Wars: One Shot at Glory
The Serbian Revolution: 1804-1835
Peace Won by the Saber: The Crimean War, 1853-1856
The Fiery Maelstrom of Freedom
The Wars of the Roses

Irish Heroes
Grace O'Malley: The Pirate Queen of Ireland
William Butler Yeats: Nobel Prize Winning Poet
Scáthach
Finn McCool